PARROTS

Sandie Lee Books

Parrots

Parrots are beautiful birds. There is around 372 different species. The first parrots date back millions of years. Today, many species of parrots have been domesticated and kept as pets. These birds can make wonderful companions; however, some species are being taken from the wild to put into the pet trade. This is dangerous to the bird. What else can we discover about the parrot? Read on to explore more fun facts about these remarkable creatures.

Where in the World?

Did you know most parrots live in tropical climates? They can be found in South and Central America, South and Southeast Asia, Africa and Australia. Parrots like the rainforests or areas with lots of trees. Here they can stay safe from predators, find food, make their nests and raise their young.

The Body of a Parrot

Did you know parrots come in all sizes? They can be as small as 3 inches in length, all the way up to 3 feet. Parrots have broad, curved bills and small black eyes on the sides of their heads. Most parrots also have very thick and strong tongues, which helps them get various nuts and seeds from their shells.

The Parrot's Features

Did you know the parrot's foot is called, Zygodactyl? This means 2 toes on each foot faces frontwards and 2 face backwards. Each toe has a strong claw on it. The legs of the parrot are also very sturdy, but they are short. The parrot's feathers can be very brightly colored.

What a Parrot Eats

Did you know the diet of a parrot varies? Parrots will eat insects, nectar, various seeds and nuts, fruit, buds and other plant material. These birds use their strong jaws to crush the seeds and nuts. Some species of parrots also eat clay for its minerals and to absorb toxins in its stomach.

The Parrot as Prey

Did you know the parrot has natural predators in the wild? Monkeys and snakes will prey on parrot eggs when the nest is left unattended. The biggest predator to the parrot is man. Humans hunt parrots for food and its feathers. The loss of the parrots natural habitat is also a cause for its demise.

Parrot Talk

Did you know some parrots can learn human speech? Some species of parrots can learn how to mimic human words. These words are usually very simple and short like, hello and goodbye. One African Grey parrot actually managed to learn over 800 words! Parrots can also whistle and will make soft clicking noises.

The Parrot's Nest

Did you know some parrots nest on the ground? Parrots do not build nests in the branches of trees. Parrots nest inside the hollow of a tree in the wild and in a nesting box in captivity. When parrots nest on the ground, they dig out a hollow in the earth.

Parrot Mom

Did you know most female parrots can have eggs at 3 years-old? Female parrots can lay anywhere from 2 to 8 eggs in one clutch. She will lay an egg every day or two until she is finished. Once all the eggs are laid, she will start to incubate them. This means she will sit on them to keep them warm.

Baby Parrots

Did you know newborn parrots look sort of like aliens? Baby parrots are born with few or no feathers at all. If they have feathers, they will be soft and fuzzy. The baby parrot's eyes are closed and it is totally defenseless. The mother parrot feeds her young regurgitated food. This special food has already been eaten and brought back up by the mother parrot.

Parrots at Rest

Did you know parrots sleep at night? When the sun goes down, the parrot goes to sleep. This is called, roosting. Some species of parrots will sleep in a large group, while others will sleep alone or with another parrot alongside. Parrots may tuck their bills into or under their feathers to get some shut eye.

Life of a Parrot

Did you know some parrots can live a very long time? Smaller parrots, like budgies, can live to be from 15 to 25 years-old. The larger breeds of parrot can live upwards of 75 years of age. Parrots spend their time, flying, searching for food and grooming themselves. Left alone in the jungles, these birds have a pretty good life.

The Amazon Grey Parrot

This species of parrot is a very popular pet to keep as a pet. It is highly intelligent and can learn to mimic sounds and words.   It is steel-grey in color, with a white face and black bill. Their loving and playful personality is why so many people want them as pets.

The Kakapo

This species is the rarest of all the parrots. It is a nocturnal bird, that cannot fly. It is the heaviest of the parrot species, weighing in at around 8 pounds. This bird was almost hunted to extinction, but has made a small comeback. It is native to New Zealand.

The Macaw

This species of parrot is perhaps the most beautiful. Its feathers can be bright blue, yellow, red, green or a mixture of all. It is a long bird that measures about 3.2 feet long from head to tip of its tail feathers. This parrot will eat clay to absorb the toxins in its stomach from poisonous seeds.

Quiz

Question 1: Where do some wild parrots end up?

Answer 1: In the pet trade

Question 2: How long can the biggest parrot be?

Answer 2: 3 feet long

Question 3: The parrot is "zygodactyl." What does this mean?

Answer 3: It has 2 toes facing frontwards and 2 facing backwards

Question 4: What is one of the biggest threats to the parrot?

Answer 4: The loss of its habitat

Question 5: Which parrot is known for being very smart?

Answer 5: The Amazon Grey

Thank you for checking out another addition from Sandie Lee Books! Make sure to check out Amazon.com for many other great titles.

www.ingramcontent.com/pod-product-compliance
Lightning Source LLC
Chambersburg PA
CBHW050802290526
45792CB00008B/2292